Radio at Night

D1613703

Books from Lunar Chandelier Press

Tiny Gold Dress by John Godfrey 2012
Earth after Earth by Toni Simon,
with drawings by the author 2012
Deliberate Proof by Vyt Bakaitis 2010
petals, emblems by Lynn Behrendt 2010
Homework by Joe Elliot 2010

Radio at Night

recent & selected work

Laurie Price

for Susan Noel,

With appreciation — "Take its kindness"
(p.28)

— love — and more,

[signature]

March 2013.

LUNAR CHANDELIER PRESS

Copyright © 2013 Laurie Price
All Rights Reserved. First Edition
Printed in the United States of America

ISBN: 978-0-9846076-5-5

Cover: "La Casa de Las Maravillas," © 2011, collage by Laurie Price

Interior photos: Laurie Price
Oaxaca, Mexico. p. xii
New York City. p. 12
Sidi Ifni, Morocco. p. 46
Barcelona, Spain. p. 66

Author Photo: Judi Price

For more information about Laurie Price see:
http://graciouseconomiesandcorrugatedshadows.blogspot.com.es
http://lauriepriceediting.wordpress.com

Book and cover design by Julie Harrison www.julie-harrison.com

Published by Lunar Chandelier Press
Brooklyn, New York
http://lunarchandelier-lunarchandelier.blogspot.com
lunarchandelier@gmail.com

for three sisters

Acknowledgments

First, many thanks to the editors of the following magazines where some of this work first appeared, sometimes in a different version: *Barbara Henning's Blogspot, The Bedside Guide to No Tell Motel - Second Floor, Big Allis, Black Bread, Can We Have Our Ball Back, Dialectical Anthropology, The Duplications, The East Village, Eoagh, E·ratio, Faux Press, Hamilton Stone Review, The Hat, How2, Ixnay Press, MiPOesias, Object, Overplay/Underdone* poetry anthology by Medusa's Laugh Press, *Peep / Show Poetry, Poems of the Virtual Island, Readme, Reciclajegranada, Shampoo, Softblow* and *Xcp.*

Then, special thanks go to the following publishers: Gary Sullivan & Nada Gordon for *Under the Sign of the House,* (chapbook, Detour Books, 1998 / readme [online, 2000]); Joe Elliot for *The Assets,* (chapbook, Situations Press, 2001) and Jack Kimball for *Minim* (Faux Press e-book, 2002). They first published some of these poems in their contextual wholes.

Neither least nor last, I want to thank the following writers and co-respondents whose various presences, through the airwaves / in absentia or not, challenged and supported me and made all the difference: Susan Edwards, Mitch Highfill, Wendy Kramer, Kimberly Lyons, Susan Noel and Albert Sgambati.

And neither first nor last but somewhat continuously, acknowledgements to Mexico, New York, Morocco and Spain, for the listening.

"If comparing a piece that is a size that is recognised as not a size but a piece, comparing a piece with what is not recognised but what is used as it is held by holding, comparing these two comes to be repeated. Suppose they are put together, suppose that there is an interruption, supposing that beginning again they are not changed as to position, suppose all this and suppose that any five two of whom are not separating suppose that the five are not consumed. Is there an exchange, is there a resemblance to the sky which is admitted to be there and the stars which can be seen. Is there. That was a question. There was no certainty. Fitting a failing meant that any two were indifferent and yet they were all connecting that, they were all connecting that consideration. This did not determine rejoining a letter. This did not make letters smaller. It did."

— Gertrude Stein, 1914, from Rooms, in *Tender Buttons*

Table of Contents

Morocco

Spain

Mexico

Minim

tion. The power inside under.
Gone the grey substitutes
or something in between.
Declaring something doesn't make it so.
The hypnoid state might
slink behind Z's frontiers
to escape the real stupor.
Some circumstance or other.
But this is where its formal beauty
lies. Some circumstance or other.
Whereas when the rain stops and sun
reappears, the cold bitten afternoon
remains. In declension. Of less value
then? What's left crowded with re
semblance drills to a center. Too fast
to be guided by a state of something that
matters. Now the truisms begin,
duplicitous by nature.

Junk

I am China, not beautiful nor waxen. The blue girl is a guest
arriving in blue light. Lateness of hour. Simple boats rock
softly to cross the spheres where all that is yellow is not light
and all that is blue isn't disappearing. Acts are hard to figure
like the odds. Lanes with no effect striate the waters, also blue.
The movement turns jerky, not dangerous, but portentous
just the same. And having no parallel. Recognition plays
the heavy in questions of access. Systematic defense
meant to brutalize the odds of no man's land. This is why
the water looks so cold. White canvas sailcloth dispatches
windy currents. No investigation of course, closer
and I slipped the large pictograms beneath the wooden
slat seat. The dumb earth won't move.

As much air or water bound by earth

as if the mantle had fallen
far from here lit in its light
And charred to loam what meant as green
The ribboned scent spread flat as air
forced under pressure to engrave
leaves an impression
Shadowy sequoia and red mudded shale
rocks loose in windward breaks
The apex dies at dusk time
Blue tree trunks line the black
on black sky

In time

Response builds a fusion of things gone stark where
circumstance dictated levels of control. Another way
to describe wind blown apart settling deep in gravity's
cling. Then, as always, night is upon us singing the
interior landscapes as they sidle overhead in mistaken
sequence. Each note corresponds to an accordion
paged codex handed over in a dream coinciding with
a Mongolian letterwriter from an earlier dream, plate
47, for which no date is given. Little is known about
them but that they were practitioners of an art that even
then had little practical application.

Think of it

Later on I know a bunch of my relatives
are coming over & I hear them arrive. I think
of it and Sam the Sham & the Pharaohs'
Wooly Bully on the radio. I go downstairs
where I lay down my head and all the parts
of the dream since I was 6 years old.
I go down to my etc. there because
a basement approach is necessary and graphic.
There are tools above a drawer labeled graphite,
refreshments behind a bar and a spicy dark corner
where I stretch the truth. Many-colored fabrics
and scraps of thread part the armchair from the floor.
I move my anchor again, stock & fluke & shank.
A hill is just landscape, an ocean spills escape.
To be lost at all an error I feel upstairs because
the expansion chamber of that liquid compass
lacks a float inside its glass dome. Walking back
& forth trying to find my stuff wakes me up
somewhere else in the middle of a sentence
I try to bring back but don't remember.

Alive

The same here naming acts of everyday
in the scheme more of itself
water being a constant.
To say it differently say it within you.
Shelf. Things which are not so
start one way can be practical or
incidental or merely at large.
It takes between that looks
likewise stretching
what you can know.

In the scheme of falling
things things get broken.

A contingency hinging on
hedges what's green.
Water that giveth funneling
unto balance without captions.
Or spills to the rescue
what sleeping does.
Listen to the greenery:
Cricket networks hissing
Kiss-blowing lizards.

Boat

A then was verse or other boat. Yes,
counterclockwise looked where a sinkhole
sunk. Pieces sting and who that smaller
said? The aisles by the something
counter stem. Some copper of my things
went black in pieces. If I liked the sake
of politeness I began another version of
the Prado. A bellowing tuba opera leading
to the larger boat. Sidetracked the hologram
closeup of putting stuff into the ideal
vacation. The obvious receive. "I control
this loss" she said, "hoist me up."

Tifoidea

I go then forcibly arguing
these medicines to wit
as clear descent squeezed
between arrangements
fundamentally triggering

Just staying far away
from what would worry
the uses of charm
like blue light hovering
to go away from then
toward a volume remembered

Likened to soiling
that which we could
and counting on cooperation
with blind desires
a mask to unravel
after seeing it chaste

Convinced of my fear
a place to start from
to burn the gestures
away from the hold
you say to me is hard
going getting lost in my stuff

Taken like that
in a word assaulted
where no agreement dwells
without effect affects
the one place we could
almost be sure of

Wonder occupies this
dismantling braceleted
between discs
of another other
what calls to be
cherished voluntarily

I believe in the body
routed into
telling thus factored
abstracts the places
I would go to
My secret longitude

Some night as time goes

lying on your back amid the swell
searching for a map in what sky
or roof or ceiling provides
or an imitation with no limitations
to the known caesuras
in some American source of opinion
     that regards the whole as a doubling
        over of its parts, not merely classical
       in its fine metonymies but attentions
pigmented as essential
in what is not one's personal concern
implies great and continuous risk
orderly as the old books of tables
become inflexible and changeless
lengthwise where the ceiling fissures
might prevent a clear view of cloud or sun
in that line separating structure from function
& to bring down the prospective offerings
might suggest a restive equivalent to
the eyes shut once more, dreaming,
possibly inching toward some kind of
breath

Windows

A tougher beyond than eyes that picture
put the sex into paint Leg of throat and
my air of above, love when dulled

introduces the tendency of
nowhere in shade
A teacup of darkest desire
that the brown spots might be hills
Where you walk must have danger
transparent in razored light

Walking as letters remembered
targets the splayed form anyone can read
from a painted surface in your head

New York

Pearl

shyness or secretiveness
in offering unwelcome criticism
employed by my industry
of backslash intervals
(titled more at lachrymal)
of basic human doubt, a theory
of reality that the mind can't frame
supposing no universal essences
that can't be blamed on a single
concept or image corresponding to
the random changes that attract attention,
a tension by which a curve intersects itself
nominates a trifling amount of fixity
evidenced by small round grains
nearly neutral slightly bluish medium gray

Postcard

Fading into someone's power to suggest before
calling to the next uneven source issues. Anywhere you go
makes a pattern & the wind, unevenly fluttering, brackish and thistled.
In this corner, and talk about it. Revenue charts.
Anywhere you go dilutes the giggles and the conference
to a tighter bring. Nighttime breaches undulated paths.
Another confidence scheme thwarts but relax, she says,
less than imagining says. At night hardly among them
and talk about it and buying. Then will ringside chanting &
prompt forgiveness. And repeats herself would be
forgiven, for instance, in segmented contrast to which
a matrix of vowels could speech themselves.
Everyone's descriptions touch one thing. Spatterbrains
in vitriol, mysterious for their assent. Push the careworn aside border
verges on lunacy. Gestures these views to an erstwhile drama
but then like small flags, see, these hands would just wave.

Loan

I'm sick with the country of this breath, a little death itself
black square in what undetected bleak hole
damn those hornblowers out on sarcastic avenue
the auguries akin to light sleep clocked
giving onto pages of an overwhelming hunger.
This flirting with universal boredom banks meretricious
shifts swift into parking lots where buses don't go.
So will you sing loudly now, several rows behind me,
to remind those dollar amounts subtracting
this intimate consumer from wishes & regrets?

State of grace

for George Albon

Here's the deal, a dream, a commutation
having not said enough yet too much so far
reveals. That three categories distinguished
could be such only in the pejorative sense
this morning at 10:17 a.m. from which
the underlying circumstances visible
at street level beyond the steely griffin
circa 1930-something proudly tilted
from roof edge to street, no pithy observation here
to hypertextualize the context from which the day,
a choir of angels swimming though a watery sky
banks, as dry breath, dependent upon the firm
that warmth is often being, stunned by tracing
the uppermost regions of a space, or space itself,
that which we once might have called,
voices once again seeping among
the registers, heaven.

Crunch

Later on we'll remember a showing of hands,
bright promise popping like dandelions
under some trees. They used to turn late
in September. But now the apple green towtruck
pulling away the boxes and broken furniture
is pulling away. All that's useful to know
but can't be used is a state of definition.
My job entails making the margins evident
to their guys while our guys crank the numbers.

Conveyance

for Kimberly Lyons

Each moment a molecule.
Shape of the resonant
blurred, with dotted lines.
Lock the fractures in
to find the fissured veins
of leaf to stem.

Dark in a language unlike
the storied, by now practical means
knowing approach to water or
car-crossed streets the bicycles
spool through is divined.
I think a street sign marks a corner
could go anywhere to traffic
with the green at the red.
Decision as division
drives away from that moment.

That moment is yours or mine
while the river pushes is pushed.
Now the full moon waxes
provocatively between
spired towers. Pushes and gusts
part the cotton curtains.
Halo round as an African sun.

Small faces boxed under glass
watch from the wall above.
The suns and moons
join to sonnet in couplets.
And charm, unlike a basket
for the next one there
their things which lyrical
and do receive.

Funnel for conveying
for conveyance a flame
the scarlet hatches
a ballerina's step-
ped into
the dominant
arrangement.

Bath

for R.S.K.

No lavender like speech to break the discontinuity
of words in jars
A present made potent as
deeper depends from some wellbeing
at the surface Struck a dowsing chord Not mine

I was in the third world
tendering an incline
to venture into

A bowl of water either calm
or inverted A mineral sachet
into which I put many many things

The whirlwind aromas troll the surface smooth

Sky speech a blue swirl
brushed by other times I knew
those fluid fictions came from
someone else's thoughts not mine

Song

    The jog and steam
that garners song, talking vast edges
to a smooth spot. All the words
are hungry to nest. Green as green
is. As jonquil is tranquil.

Orphaned

I enter the doctorate of time. An interpretive opera.
The bellows refract, south of where words have been
called writing, legs up on the table, hands clutched
in a fist. First this spell of something terrible weaving
in its course, then a large mass under the moon's maria.
I put it lightly. To reward that kind of theory weathering
all manner of dislocation. A thing averted. A zone that's
pure paleomagnetism. Magic. Magenta. Foundling.

Smoke

the physical which is not logical
scrap that and start again
the physical which has and is
capacity, human body & its ways
in the art of assembling, dance and frame
left as is or was, capacity, and gathering
strength or accumulating grace
met by left as is or was

someone depends on that

this detour that thinks this detour is thinking

must begin again, take a stand, brave
determination and failure
to balance a coordinate
relax the drones

intervention reversing the ceiling which had
had, pale color respirating
after edges stack of buildings
had come, were going

it was the best of times the worst of times
fawn disorder   young private issues quelled

one single dwelling
dog for its dog
January's curious plan museum

Pages of a done book

I sat strange enough to alone-start the lens. Moreover the getting had heart, was a complete and perfect survival. We made love. We climbed exploring the packed-in backbones of the books. Seduction of birthmark an inch from the lens. From my eye for transfixion calls for skills in the hands of those who have gladness. I read settled in stake chapter. Coffee is my friend. My audience was water, hand slaked to tap. Returning to some otherwise that no one else could claim.

One sign to learn the formula I fed on so the street's parallel wouldn't violence as figures of speech compromised past. A before only depicted the signal lights. The mind shed its leaves, traced the way an age is told to gauge the rebuilding embryo. In other words, imagine.

He spoke the hypnotic "listen" – a link to cluster the contour maps. To feed apart the sense points, the line, its silhouettes. Grasping and chasm; wings and the poem. What saves us he said is no vision, no visible control. The isolations know the facts and complex neurons made synthetic. Hearing trumpets I said the hearing trumpets.

Words as artifice, breakage, mistakes. Rub the tall consonants to build an alpine fire and trace the shapes of the trees with your fingers and hands. Make the theatre rise to a standing ovation. A house was invention itself, these ovals your birthright – their tridents like dandelions.

The wind dies. Bronze clasp, glass lines. Women paint their eyes open on the street of middle ciphers. Decibel levels of squall undress the deaf pistils and itinerant sun dates your actions from the pages of a done book. Eyes, horizons, advancing to cities visible beyond the ruckus.

Thoughts in trains, on trains, landscapes pulled away. I owned more than one narrative able to live in a person. Could do the invention stories. Could do the juries hung on fascination. Appearance inside the single aesthetic could chance there and it was ripe. Audience of intelligents.

Pronouncements clashing at the console. By nightfall the permissions gave way to unstructured cobalt portals. Internal spheres out for a spin. Moving my lips along the middle range carried the tunes above the rudiments.

You go along pasting the narrative to each [p]age as if knowledge is social. More knowledge against bumping up against. Ravaged where anonymity hangs like summer heat. Bogged down by cigarette object an oral shape recites dark sonnets. The elements emit. I liked that and bathed in its glow. Toasted enzymes torched by long blue rocks of vapor.

Periodic spring the cozier lines. *Tirar*, to pull; *empujar*, to push. Hinge spread and tool kit, sprocket for the host. Coercions shaped a place for the mix. Swapping meant mapping, bound the wholes in their synapse. Notes on personal convention in lieu of smashing through but in so much feedback a motor motions caution.

I kiss you in my thoughts love, suppose the transformations sans your dynamic. Simulated knots knocked out the connections. This is my everything, my beginning, my now.

History falls outside like snow

for Susan Noel

History falls outside like snow. Pick a picture. Take your pick.
Bent surfaces catch raking light. Slow dissolve, wrinkled purl.
No sudden moves and no one gets hurt. Spool your kindness
closer to the light where we can feel it. What brings you to
this necessity blur? Business or vacation? Own or rent?
Make an intelligent decision. Pick a color. History falls
outside like snow. Take its kindness. No one gets hurt.
Big chunks of mental tissue spool like decisions.
Pick your membrane. Light dissolves hurt places
in its sudden blur. Haunt your vocation 'til it be
seen. Necessity colors each surface with intelligence.
Lines up the pictures. Pools the dissolved.

A symmetry

Imperative behavior isn't said
or spoken nothing's open when
impassive words clustered & broken
rape the luxuries of & accuse
an absence of color risen in waves
I pause here against a blank
palette as a Japanese gesture
to balance, shiver the last curtaincall
one of us is thinking
and small white flowers
divided by seeds from this world
where life must blend vertically
when it keeps being the same
sense of negotiation, white threads
held resistant to the repetition of
'no further danger speaks in right speech writ'

Glow worm

Someone unstained from the previous fragment risk.
Furtive wisdoms freckled over and browed in amber light.
Brown match of magazine and filter, a way of retrieving
some facet. But cold stands hijack promise, belated
strands of thought sump where now here is nowhere.
A little glow worms its way to through you.
Some premium. Some spark.

Bank

oh god thy art may hearten
incoming messages ordered
to road & leaves made fragrant
and temple, a slow currency
in cash-fast deals whose lobes grant
some protection where the problem
is wrinkles or hidden by clouds.
Hidden by clouds I found myself.
I found myself in Asia with a sound
idea and a garment of glass
carriaged largely by photographs
outside the camera's range & no plans
or modern landscape to race toward
but a backdrop of palms to be pleased
with. It was the emptied eye a dwindling
of assets the sign of casings cracked
underfoot. The sparkling coins there
blinded me best. But I saw no soldiers
nor reference to hands.

Trick

Breathing fills the air modules in a slipstream of flurry.
Events staked to the young private boom of city
and mind alight on notions of sleep this night
embodies. Massive ideas rake you forward.
Nonsense vowels extend toward an order
that fascinates upon waking but that comes later.
No vacancy sign aflutter is seen by a lamp.
Even the subtle slips slip by where a smile
realignment bursts to take place. I've been had
a little thought we could pass around, wording.

Radio at night

eventually future retains my other
subject to imagination the story I do
now at night, whispering fan
and the green radio light

what's purple is a golden crescent
in a black sky suspended between
the bridges where I carry forward
to write alive the lines or be still

later white windmills of sleep
power the leaves of dreaming
a tree & future retains my other
radiant light where it sings

Chinese spaces

Red carlights fade up the street to write away the sentence as it would go away, attached still to others' lips conscious of subject and context. This kind of negative space, any inscription and the why factor mesmerized by a mental state. I inebriate myself. The reflexive din. Restaurants play German MTV and my doctor has a new plan. To play with ideas has an interesting design but I'd prefer to design the interest. Test the severity from a blind corner crucial to the dogmatic. Hop to where it comes from, so it could go, accumulating details.

Accumulating details the work ahead. Vast staircase in a building with lush interior balconies, its black dome taunting and electric. What sonic precursors floated this music? drill into Chinese spaces struggling to reconcile the shifts that bring us here? What's novel is how the hazy areas point out the ragged weave of situation trust. Friends in dreams dance out from the spirals. E-merge as if the business were commerce and what I'd find there could fortune. An afternoon storied by damp yellow penmanship in the waiting room grid. Clouds pass in a drone of white rhythm, blinding, severe. A stark build of aerial views to bless the grey sky as if lit from behind by their own pale light.

By their own pale light, by whatever means necessary, by their musics spoked around a single note sustained and the endless paragraphs traced with precision from here to there. The thing inside the thing inside. A half-time subscription turns back the clock from imagination. Everybody's trumpeting is perfectly material and as such, bores the narrative to a talkative halt. Years still worth counting counter the overall design. Unlike these epigrams bordering the divined.

Tick

Starts with a transliteration of mercy, dark blue aggregate, ticking at the stripped breeze. A singular word that means impossible. Blink. Culls a sequence at the edge of an eyelid. To fight against sight and its proprietary counsel dictates another field of composition, or composure alters the importance of. In certainty there is modesty, the wide breeze fully correcting. A knowing sureness governed by slippery cobalt deposits, who knows where awakes. And though the texture weaves in horizontal bands, another oversight, day pushes on toward day where reflex bent forward as if in meditation defers.

The body politic

Wind high velocity turns the sky from darkness toward another kind of darkness.
Where guarded fabrics clothe clouds form the lazy definitions. And whether
or not looks immaterial from this angle this talk of angels. Wings I said as
if speaking of gossamer. The miraculous things are easy to describe once
you set them down at table's edge to get better acquainted. I have this history
swallowed whole you could say down pat. I wasn't always used to it. Any heaven
lodges complaints. Though by and by a large thing seeks to clarify or rise
spellbound to pare down the options. Human nature runs its force of habit
but if you call it come toward it narrowing. To speak its name. To name its
speech, a kind of thread hanging loose in a light drizzle sprinkling *chipichipi*
in a tongue tasting describes. The radar of anyone's instinct witness to voice
what might be supposed, though jumping through conclusions tastes rain or
the lingering scent of its arrival for a magnet to lure. To take then. Speaking
of skill wills the odds in my direction and I'll have no more availed myself of
the powers than if chosen. Oh be a chosen one said the blonde acquaintance
choosing to observe that something could grow there some thing could glow.

Tintoretto's profile

Take on a profile in the Venetian scrim. Let the air inside
your hair. A small amount can be cautioned or controlled
but if the push slips you're just a mineshaft away from being someone
else's fun. No need to laugh when laughter's grim. Like when you
stood back to let those dogs run past and
each one slowed to sniff. I didn't egg them on.
You can't collar a victim every time so go home
to your drugs and striptease. A gracious arm spreads the way
a body is cruel extravagance looks to be seen seeing each day. Then
the hands begin to sing. Impulsive stretch of little finger perpetrates
my heart's stutter beat. But even after all this
I won't believe the smaller gesture's
the one I want.

Bird, plane, apostrophe

Park the ribbons of feeling
and trees

Lean away from the massed sky of motion,
way of poetic filter, words' weight that waits
to line the banter with something
more than punchy lit crit

A park for your enemies
if stopping,   finally,   you find you
have made some

Or be some other property about which
no one has knowledge

joke of hollow text
surface to complete disappearing

Every little wonder that is address–
Sense of safety or sedation–

Someone's always watching
out their window
in a sinkhole or sledged
right down peeking
out between the trees

There's a mirror audience beckonable
by beeper by cellphone
Bird   plane   apostrophe

Grand concourse

for Albert Sgambati

I was seated by the window humming to myself. The plane left and we flew
hard. Several landings later it was night. Loaded all my boxes onto a truck
headed east. Smoky colors of smoke-free view across the plains, steamy
afternoons barreling across agricultures and some ancestors' playgrounds.
Not mine – my people barged in as pleasure-seekers in their century. Never
learned to talk right. Note the greener than green of how green was her valley.
Grand concourse of brown cow-lined road through birdshit-spattered
windshield points toward first sightings of motels and stars. Venus and Mars
visible through flat Midwest truckstops with showers and all-you-can-eat
buffets. Ohio, wide as remembered and Pennsylvania more. Told that a high
percentage of sitting cows signal rain I post my sights on the clouds. My
grandmother's sing-song 'e'-flected 'i' in beau-ti-ful spoken by the man at the
wheel. Stop and go across GW Bridge's giant pearl necklace exaggerates into
schools of horns and scratch-beat mufflers: New York, self-contained continent
of itch. Rectangles thin sky. Birds trinket wires.

White noise

About ten minutes goes by in the hunting frame. By the arrows rising from
the grass I see the main stem. Flotilla of shadows. Then a cloud rolls over to
reveal the sun. To be lifted at such an angle from the city's rough ledges balances
a lull in the discussion. I begin with a retraction. I begin the same way I have
for the past who-knows-how-many years. I grab my beer off the sidewalk and
take a swig. The need for type O blood is constant, broadcast over all available
airwaves. Hold my breath as the liquid warms threading down. The engines
turn slowly at first, their movements barely perceptible. But let me go back
and explain: my sense of 'the' truth is 'my' own. For this reason I begin having
become as it were.

Smoke from a cigarette left in an ashtray rolls and unwinds in slow motion.
As quickly as the smoke overtakes the room the sheer silence is faster. Point
of entrance for nerve fibers and cells to dissolve. This numbing pulse of
loss is sensate and octagonal climbing along thin strands of nerve release
to collect in the nuclei. A pale blue verging on gray petals through the room
unmoored. The fresh damp aroma sparks recognition, palpable as earth. Ah
sweet sweet sweet September. The warning and the reprimands; the smoke
wavers in a thick column not settling for days until the rains come. You
chase it to there: your grief darkens in flames of boxed conclusions. Where
steam rises from the frame the long thoughts bubble. Durations of octaves
grounded by middle C.

The next frame holds a pattern of circulars.

Into the irregular patterns of rectangles and squares I walk a cobblestone path to search for the Plaza of the Inquisition. The ground is uneven or falling rising slanted at various degrees. Torqued. Feel the tension rise from cement patches and the voices of others passing. "We live in trailer wipe. We live in ashen stage ashram noise." The whispered solace of solitude joined to dead voices echoes. Never in negation was the thing more than. Lines of sunlight vibrate between buildings.

(Once late at night I saw white owls fly from one bell tower to the next to the next to the next. But this afternoon there are only groups of men and women inking old metal presses to spool out invitations or business cards, examples of which hang from the sides of their machines.) I am cheated of your tomorrow says the postered plea for mercy. ". . . wearing a red T-shirt, a large silver cross . . . has a raised mole above left eyebrow."

Whenever we could we came there to delay the disappearing. She said if it wasn't one thing it was two. Hedged all our bets to defray the tumble of torn edges from forming any kind of line. A beseechment to startle the revelers from their broken bits of talk and salutations. The revised revise, the risen rise. We mourn the dead. We speak of them fondly that we might occasion them. Them as yours as if your own. The borders I drew on that pane of glass propped against the windowframe were just an amusement. What I meant was that there could be more than one way to address an infiltration. It would be a tight squeeze to fit the location structure to the place point and without directions the best I could do was improvise. (To look inside the grief: the little waves and tendered manias.)

The constants are the flux and drone of car alarms when a bus rushes past. Music yells through big speakers into autumn rooms, which, lush as leaves swept into piles, star brittle textures anointing. Then the proteinaceous drugs kick in. A muse of sucks. Brittle elements shift to tactics sometimes. Sometimes sleeping reasons are enemies. Who polishes their cross, their knife, its blade.

Trails and tangents are set and reset by footsteps wading through sagebrush and pine needles, leaves and clumps of hair. Girl with big feet nestles cornered in a camphor smell rising from a coat closet stuffed with notes. Fur drips slithering out from the cracks in arpeggios. The patter of tropical rain lingers while two strangers stop midstep in the street below to check their notes. Two sets of wet hands carefully unfold the papers. Clouds drift overhead uncertainly, clearing and boxing together to drift like smoke. Treetops appear blackened in the wet, slice through thick mist in waves. From here I see an open door weathered green in places, moss-hung drapings.

Strings that reverberate against a cherry wood backboard lend an air of solemnity to the occasion. Piano and slow. *Controvoglia.* That music could be tamed this way in trills or
rising gestures

> to complete the narratives inside
> was nourishment enough.

That what was expected would come to pass, that what could be hoped for would follow. The notes droned sinuous to deepen the paved distributions of the flattening tones. There was a restless fumbling around for keys that might have seemed human considering the divisions but the molting structures worked against it and the tuneful hollows assumed their positions.

An infinite approach to an infinitive will always begin with "I." Then I could stand back and watch as the day folded into quadrants of multiples, assume my position at the head of the line.

I bound cords around papers trying to separate those that had been read from those that hadn't. A slipknot seemed the logical approach. Heaving line, clove hitch. The stacked edges threaten to topple away from assembling.

If you study any part of a sequence too long the connections fall away and gravity seems to cease. The sky becomes a dense blue smudge drawn across the top of a window and hung there instead of glass. But if you turn around quickly and let the image fall into place by itself its attention to logic resumes as if no separation of belief had taken place. At the laundromat when the dryer won't respond to the coindrop or button push: You're there again it says. You've never been closer. That was what I strove for. Whirling helped to diagram the steps this dancer might take to lose the static equations.

New York

"Cross the black lines of intrusion"
thinking I would rather alone than not
Brisk permutations of an address made
odd is the party we would drive to
withhold the false notwithstanding
desire pronounced distinctly and hard
like fuck

Epigraph

This here is now. I lean in, I walk the august
rocks of passage, tremendous rendezvous of
tightened inquests, I descend the staircases of
rude basements, navigate between the rusted
pipes of belief. And I seat myself down,
forever down where it is always now, where a
twinned nanosecond blows persistently
through the cracks. And the slamming of the
shutters never stops, nor the dust-infused air,
nor the concussion of glass with cement that
goes on pounding and smashing and never
breaks.

Morocco

Wind & sea

Each anticipation, each creature a house,
the bread of house, surface crayons
a deeper exchange, wild sky rippled like tongues,
bystander of criticals. Chalkboard texts and bags
and bags of shells rendered to chalk
as each wave recedes. Have something
the paper wonders wanting to have
something other than ink, hands
cradled under chin and face above.
Can I have the obsessive details please. Always
the wind, another kind of monster. Unglazed clay
floor seeps moisture and why not say it
calms the nerves to sit here. Now. Capital.
A better like than no stains of previous mixtures
makes a better sharp. The point of falling down
and finding windows. My sole to my soul a wry
idea with no conclusion. Fold the paper money.
The grain of that becoming, unlike artifice
sees each passing cloud seize the eyes
untied, the eyes to sea with, unite,
exchange beneath the deep, poems
coiled inside bottles, barnacled dance
of treasure among sparkled and domed
waves. A mistress of beginnings flaunted,
favoring the script of sea creatures
vaulted from the riptides of
a tremendous force pulls
the lobbying words
to bob and surface,
shimmer like sardines.

What's ugly

Forget ink, butter, or warm things.
A sneeze in full air the goshen of,
and door slams shut that gravity pulls.
Inside are the clever tricks this day
bought for one final gain. To sponge
the materials begs another signal & share
in the latticework of a metal sheared
under the din of its music. Alone or not
the lah-di-dah hummed in yellow keys
and crowds call out the titles as they pass.
This one evidenced and that one
breaks apart. Red sweater at dusk. Wind
would laugh as bird is animate brushing only
at the tip. A small reminder of size
and frequency, weight and buzz. Endless
modifications make up the urge of throat
in gasp in dry approximations pencilling
classical complaints to the extremes
as refuge. Garishly painted houses
outside all means of survival means
what's ugly survives without exclusions.

It costs

Why not go inside I'm saying
What we were before this wind
and our sentences cut short
A life sentence to animate and people
with trees or boats and so many names
narrowed in to shifting shapes
but not arrowed down in transience
and so on and so forth
There's enough space to be and let this
in and watch as space comes unexpected
and challenges, to be and let these things
wash over, dissolve
I go to truly enter the fluid
not concrete of these things that go
on moving barely in one place, palace
before the other things trespass
Tiger cat puddled between chair legs
knows this passage too,
how to get there   is   it costs
To be present and alive like breath
A line of permanence in perpetual resolve

Waves

to be in the foreign body as a luxury
of clandestine presence so only in my
apparent absence which is hidden but
shifted from the always there to
sometimes comes, sometimes stays,
sometimes goes alone to the beach
to walk inside the tidal atmosphere
and thick air, blowing sand & seagulls,
attributes of a resting place gaze, gazelles,
and let the words drift or sift as worlds
I'm coming into in a slow repose
to hear the sounds caught in their
throats as birds as language as bent
between the spaces I can imagine
if I keep my mouth closed & just listen

You

Today I saw you again. You seemed to float past the shops in a black djellaba heading towards the Place. In your hand you carried a rectangular straw market bag. You did not wear a headscarf and your long curly hair moved with you as you walked in new leather sandals on the tiled street. It was Sunday. There were some tourists exiting the corner market. ¡Que linda! one of the women said, pointing at your feet. I sat outside his shop waiting for water to boil for tea.

There was light rain and fog rolling in from the ocean. You were in a light shawl strolling towards the port. I saw you pull your cellphone from your pants pocket. The seagulls clustered over the ramparts next to the outdoor fish grills behind you. A Berber trio dressed in white djellabas with grey stripes were singing and playing at the sunset café. When they finished their song one of the men upturned his *bendir* and went from table to table collecting coins. You shook your head as you strode past. Your red hennaed hair flamed against the drab grey sky over the medina and everyone turned to look as your hair dazzled past.

Essaouira

"He talk about his father. Let me tell you about the man comes down from the mountains. He pass the little stream, you know the water running soft where the gurgles echo." He arrives in the old city, passes through the open archways to the largest plaza in the world, the Djma El F'na. "Here. Take." Take what his father tell him.

We're born with the angels by our side. The good one, who see all the good we do, the sweet, on the right shoulder; the one who see the bad, the wrong, on our left. All is written before your life begin. Each act, each way we're loving; each time we're incorrect, the false. Always they see us and the angels they judge. All of it. Written.

This man, he was solds the grass. When he catch the cops they ask what he do in this life, he tell them, 'me, I sell the plants of the god.' What can they do? They tell him he can't be do that no more so now he sells the sweet air. The old man steps up into the small shop, swings a smoking metal incense burner back and forth holding his arms out to each of its corners, chanting.

To eat with the right hand, always the right. We doing it this way. *Laf duk* (god he protect you). And the ants, we can't kill the ants or step on them. We doing it like this. They too, sacred. We can only maybe put some water, like this. His hand sweeps the air in a gesture like sprinkling. He inhales deeply from the *sepsi*. This can't think to me nothing even. I'm so far of that. It says something says. This can't touch to me that something, the perfume, the talking. I'm so far of that. What the sentence uniques. All the balance threads to matter real. It's natural. You need you let the sentence here. That salt. This earth.

About him the Essaouira wind is constant and the sea too today where he sits in his shop and in answer to a question about what he's thinking, replies 'only the good,' crosses his hand over his heart, murmurs 'hmmm?' Among the folds of Mohammed's woolen garment a kitten was born so cats are sacred. He scrubs the tea tray with a length of unraveled rope and washing powder above a partially cracked manhole cover in the street outside his shop. Nearby is the bread bakery cat, Mimi, who's pregnant again. This is the third time, that I know of. The last time she had five kittens who lived in a cardboard box outside the bakery in a wooden cart pushed up against its stone wall. They mostly slept piled one on top of the other. 'We livin' like this. Like clams,' he says. On his way home after closing his shop he buys scraps of meat and chicken in the market for them, walks all the way back to the shop to leave the open plastic bag on the ground close to the bakery door. Wool is sacred. All scraps kept. Bread is sacred. Witness the moldy piles of old baguettes for sale at the second-hand market. Grapes are sacred. I imagine the grapes as the tears of those who suffer. 'Everyone suffers,' he brags. 'There is much art.' And kilos of grapes. Day and night, hundreds of wild cats roam the streets searching for food or sit close to half ripped-apart plastic bags of garbage, licking themselves, licking the fur of their young.

Plaintive complaint snarls out a speaker followed by handclap chop chop cuts to beggar's moans. Corner cats sleep heaped, Mimi mama and her six tiny reasons. Fish heads and ash riddle tile slabs but get licked. Wooden

animal sculptures stand guard at the entrance to the shop. Inside, symmetrical carved wood couplings line the perimeter along the floor. Nshara, wood dust; Njara, wood shavings. Threads back to the music, light blink like rain. A fast drift to be nowhere in the *gnaoua* night begins again and again, each phrase lit by tune then stretch, the music lengthening towards trance.
Your red things are your artifice   You get sick from that veneer
The muezzin sings when because he must and the time for that's now.

At the port there are boats and shells of boats and shells. The walls are shell mosaics. The afternoon is slowly lowing. Behind me an oud loves its crooked scale. My head is filled with seagulls and song. The gulls mark the deeper blue surface where the water is cool. White skid narrows west. The gulls complain or coo, dipping through the surface. Hot white sun in a pale blue sky. Water lit by milky surface slow reflection. These machines to take us there to here. That invention. To be here. This elevation.

A guy walks into an antiques shop with a radio under his arm wanting to sell it to the proprietor. The proprietor unplugs his boombox and plugs in the radio in its place. It lights up, a long horizontal white band and two small circles of blue light to one side of the dial. It's a 1970s model short wave radio, German, five or six inches wide, and about 25 inches long, so it would receive bandwaves from all over the world says the guy. The proprietor toys with all the buttons, pressing each one, turning the dial this way and that. But there is no sound. Nothing. Not even static. He says, 'the radio doesn't work.' The man selling it whispers, 'but it has blue light.'

And less even to be unkind

the scrubbed appearance of certain evasions like
was but isn't now and the ragged edges
consequent as being a margin fed out
from the hollow the rattled echo shouldering
more than weight and the next one

that next straggled choice whining
is no competition for initial shocks

blurred edge, faint outline of just what
creamy blend of sharpness and blue
that erotic something once was

this fucking this   a century of
doubt and perspiration, premonition
okay but claims no experience
of prudence and less even to be unkind

reasons float like white lily pads
at the center, intussusception

I make a margin of my skin
to fit through an unobservable loophole
and disappear the masks   Is that hate?

Then force the picture cloth overhead

it draws a crowd. Sun spirals in and sand
there is sand again. Slivers shiver in light.
Always more light matched by bronze
cannons and fortification spires a skinny young boy
says something funny and laughs. Clic clic
is time passing (camera shutter) tendriled as waves
of heat the noon sun gentles down. Burn a thought
escapes. Walks the length of beach in a shimmer.
The town is a city ringed in sand and nervous
gulls circling. The dead and otherwise gone
behave. Water pushes fast as sudden
as risen tide light brown bubbles. Nubbed
by flies that bite welts skin red & starts
the associations again. Past engagements
loss factors to a single power squared. Strand.
This put of this foot in this shoe to walk
frail in heat where sodden air weighs
like a mirror's unfamiliar face. Undulation
a once-thin line. Unduration. Some be
tweens rise as minarets reply with birdlike
grasp of where they've been.

Slower than thought or vision you say

it's where the light stands, a march of
sheerest colors 'til you reach the one
that opens   Not the pale blue or grey
outline but softness like wood and tawny
almost old   The glisten over fingers curled
cooking mint tea over gas flame near a door
Silk does that too or sequins in wind   Jump
the rope black surge where details play you
for a spoon   Now the shine bowls an oval
deposit almost mineral so succinct   It's not
what you think or how your feelings craft
what you see that someone's voice
interrupts but the ambiguities come
inside and staking claims suffers
nothing to the known places
that weaken in plain sight
our bedouin eyes

Money

My poem Laurie is my poem
as perpetual here as anywhere else.
My poem is wind & red
Mogador Gaz tanks stacked
on blue wooden hand truck
on the Place Moulay Hassan,
basketball punched caught & thrown back
two children just like anywhere
in shorts & sneaks.
Someone sings in Maghrebi
what sounds like
"who rules the money?"
More coffee please at the café outside
under blue & white striped umbrella, perpetual sun.
Orange gear is popular, pants
t-shirt, sequined *baboush*, etc. This is my etc.
to take an inspiration with its larger circumference,
horizon of a bag, zero.
That's putting myself there, okay.
This close range & I still felt
the sudden violence quality
of life issues. Shadows condemned
to one side or the other
also perpetual as this is my etc.
Tourists arrive in waves of
sun appearing through cloud
always present tho' sometimes unseen
like the women here behind veils

who stripped of visible definition
offer sudden hurried glimpses
of nose & mouth but in the hammam
through steam under bare bulb light
I see Menuda, my former landlady
step towards me fat, laughing, naked
breasts & tight wet white underpants
to kiss me both cheeks.
Then we simultaneously clasp our hands
to our hearts in the Moroccan fashion
but this is not fashion, this is art, this survival.
A deeper kindness, *hanan*, means
all that is necessary is given
because this is how, location,
this where & this for what.

I plot the day around these availabilities
if that word can draw them in
& if not there's the harbor & poems.
February in Essaouira, Morocco is
wind, rain, and cold
d'bob, shta', d'brd.

After the rain sea heaves heavy
salted breath and everything smells
like pee pee *de gato,*
a white vegetable
that tastes like a box.

I pound iron nails with a big stone to hang pictures.
There is kindness in every core.
A yogic clove. Remember you're
coming to a point you don't want
hammered. Tramp through littered market streets
to the same souks as always singing
"who's got the money?" under my breath.
A fraction of nothing,
bardic despair without conjecture
& I know perfectly well that prayers
blow just like wind
sweeps tide.

Another morning prickles cold then sun through clouds
wakes the birds the passengers sleepwalking
through the train of place, terrain, and
why not face that the biggest space is
inside going up and down.
Ana mushkil kebirma bzeftl mashakil
as if a thought could be trained
or eye or 'I' it's as if I were here
to hear the sun lope across the plaza
calmly setting shadows at a tilt. Take some of that
wordlessness to let the powers reach in.
The bicycles the flies the wind again and
my dark glasses keep other silhouettes inside.
I order coffee broken with milk, *m'hersa.*

I dream a cat coming in but I don't want a cat coming in I want a word. Lean forcefully into the wind it makes a special sound. Cat coming in and birds are words or words are birds. I dream a future behind me and its past, continuing. The ocean inside and the ocean beside are perpendiculars apropos of nothing but I said so. I have no hat; I have no home. Chipped cup on a broken table, scotch tape, velcro and silicone. So much work(s) to make it stick. Catalog coming on & cats coming in. Spirals inscribed. Entirely local. Outlined.

Simple things like milk and dates, raisins and almonds, until it makes a paste and can be formed into something. The six-fingered musician sings what sounds like "who needs the money?" Going under in a small valley rivers the fear, round as coins. Those oval things that scrutinize the past from this pass.

Love poem bound by object and flame

when what feels steady and silent
focused on what as what is or not
and paper perimeter of actual space
lifts wind slams shutter door pushes
and though not evident could knit
the soft tissue how you might see
the inside of your thought but ahead
is a vast action of orange and red
and this slow speed to focus vexes
without need of attention or care
it's just there

Bienvenido

From the reticulated table of senses hovering
above a white scrim to weave the words
as plows, work the shoulders of tobacco
like leaves The seeds of questions are very small
and there's a tan for some of this tenancy
taking its time A postcard penned nets what
bottleneck does to squeeze the legible line
break thin To break the eye or laugh aloud
lets go *yala* "let's go!" they say here
locking my door in this somber port town
& a Mona Lisa moment in the mirror
descending the stair feeling
the eyes move

Spain

Cargo

I hear "no perfect unions"
and that otherness is still
there   there's a way to be
with it between it
or under the spell
of its sticky green aperitifs

Things stuck in their domains
complicate the algorithms I hate.

My favorite music
feeds its own infinitive
revisions when the violence
of a moment's sweat hosts
the audience spun inside out

To give back
and front between
receiving is riveting.

Then I'm back in my room
and feel the room well
in me too.

Liquid suitcase

That beach is place and thing, parsing active in its blanching weight, state of techno music backgrounds the locations for gathering, more than ten planets for each single grain of sand she said, late one night. Late at night the stars beach in sky, as above so below, and the pull has a name, a nexus, a white sound like a book, written distinctly in sky white letters on specific blue beyond, let's call that deeper, which is up, not down.

Call it astroglyph or expunge the theory drops lit by wet light, air of soft crystal, how everything turns, moves thinking was a war, was when was a war, wards off the eye and ear intelligences, obvious fondness for grand gestures and a thing that's of, not complete in itself or self suggests by evacuatory measures, social constructs prevalent in the inclusive, rope. Strands broaden the lengths we've come to know as conclusions but.

What I'm thinking of is questions.
The sentences begin. The sense of some arrangements, if not exactly actual, in the ways of ordering torqued interrogations. What I'm thinking of. Questions. Designed as wholes to embrace a kitchen logic beyond a sunny plastic bowl painted with cornflower blue daisies and on hand-painted ceramics embedded into outer walls of white stucco houses.

A wall, a window, a bird. Beach. Single grains unpearled. Times spent in frequented zones narrated by air. Durations. Disambiguations. Sounds track spliced frequencies. "Do you come here often?" chimed late one night. Night latens the hour.

Traveling light begs no patch of ground beneath feet. Of ground it could be said and blah blah blah concurrent with so many known things, a frangipani tree fragrants the garden that's anyone's imagination with six tender new shoots.

Later leaves. Liquid suitcase in perpetuity. Errant devotions to stars, their navigatory insistence, to frank occasions called this day or some other. Of occasions let it be said, etc. stet.

The maps are what you suspect so fold them into their drawers, zippered suitcase pockets, crux. Light travels and the speed of things.

Liquid suitcase needs no zippers. Monday, half empty, Tuesday, half empty, Wednesday, half empty, Thursday, half full. Liquid suitcase goes anywhere. Liquid suitcase is portable mass, floods the atlas, puddles between journeys.

"Faster" she said, anxiety catching up to her. Little gold reams stacked by the dozens. And the light there, tubular bulbs above a wooden table, glues and fixatives separated into a shallow cardboard cigar box on a surface called work. Tools nestle in a place called home.

This making is necessary, crests to receive open aesthetic scripture.

Translation wave, breaker, with morning foam suggesting. I learned that a little could be a lot, and that to love a sonata compounds irrelevance. Rapture.

But beach now and those grains of sand like stars stuck in all the between places and also covering the bottoms of the bottoms. Floor, seductively unfixing rolls away or toward or hewn its breathing forms graduating.

Entering involved slipping past the vital signs monitors registering horizontal blanks. People in the spreads. Odd surfaces offering explanations, names, addresses, and the habits driven by attracted attentions. The rich could find their radios here, worn hip pockets behind their smiles. Thought gash on forming skin, blood torn in a curved red stripe. Stripped down by something basic, to something basic. The hands on top of the head. Level.

But interventions of silence, or similarly, the silence of interventions, bear the larger volume of misunderstandings. Dawn is coral with Venus starring, and Bach. In this dawn-shaped light color seems significant as voice or presence hesitant to punctuate. All sentences open to more or less, the self-imposed ones usually more. And the focus of the target is what, exactly?

Distance shoulders embroidered anticipations, and though a plane is imminent there's no substituting time for space.

This language or that, it's the hands at rest that hint at larger questions. Beyond. Gestures. Always. Why?

Does this exit ramp go anywhere in particular or is the point solely to leave where you've been?

The shape and tone of a different note signals
to molecule
span of movement
indirect
flowering.

When you reach the open bar, upper octaves stilled, lower octaves trailed behind in the distance, do you rest or order a drink?

We toast our exile. The English-speaking world penetrates all alphabets, shaded orange or purple on the open map. The table is simple, the waiter sympathetic.

In the plaza beside us two gypsy vendors pack fruits and vegetables to close for the day, stack large pomegranate-laden green plastic trays inside a white van. All of this taking out and putting back echoed around the table, now peopled with two new faces and someone getting up to leave.

Freedom from obligations, implied in other obligations, the master tone of one's own voice heard above the many.

When negotiations of spirit necessitate belief and more why. Not. Imagination touches flinching mercuries. Translucent as water / color of sky. Even textiles streaking wind between buildings do describe. Red paints shout, territorial but benign because imagination dissolves, water on cloth, fingerprints on glass. Patina'd orbs flaunt their pigments.

Content versus context, treatment as subject, dangling modifiers flutter thin breezes above the plaza around that white plastic table. That sun streamed through windblown leaves sketches no pattern attests to something random.

Another round, inkling, another attendance spun from hieroglyphic representations. Can a vertical line stand in for not yet, not now?

Beach laid out along the horizon gives the sense of a reachable point in the distance. A distinction that asserts its dark slash between two paler ones, mirroring. Arms outstretched. Level.

Remote

A cologne named Siesta or
a bus route dubbed Beethoven
misplace the detachment of
solo distances from the getgo
When I hit this green button
there you are a field of mirrors
I reference the discontinuities:
to write and engage by love
& money desires impulse,
concentrated persistence
sometimes though not
altogether, almost
that

Subjunctive

Succumbed to, unlike the weight of maybe
this activity confused me sitting in a room
shy of roughly contraband minutes between
here and a plane, fog, luminous halos so
the body goes to the mine, sudden violence
of silence raking pages of hills and if one's
complications are so simple why isn't that
one this one? Neither cloud nor entrance
Noir night and moon's faint stain
scrieve someone's voice insinuating
what just passed through my head
in a tongue hesitant, wholly riven
by unease

Casino of the muses

In your figures I'm thinking
the innocence of a man
I'm engaged around the figures
putting their dreams up on the walls
When figures dance with stray winds
theoretical comparisons between
all to be done does do or maybe make
a frantic division   diverges   irrigates
squared themes solutioned by
and riddled obtains an idea
that Florence in Galileo's day
was a quest for elegance
Each sphere accepting
the yoke of its joys
would be consumed
within ten years
The ground there too was thin
Sun-baked countryside spent
Margins leaving their mark
The road when they left the permits

Voiceover

Nazanin, template for a festivity of names
returned from one continent to her native city
bedeviled by excess or dissociated from capital.
California billboards flaunt painted muscles and
birthmark close to car windows by desert's edge.
Tunnel of choices practically beside the point,
dogs bark at other dogs locked inside a lot.
Brassy radio apparition in New York taxi
briefly unwires the conceptual timeline
and spindly voiceover waves the future in,
blanks, sudden as north star and half moon
glint in whole sky striped between
buildings. Now the radio's beautiful
four syllable transmutable praise
for god, whispers.

Done

If we limit ourselves
to mending the winch
and drive the immovable
so to surveil it
only rips the cable
then we move back
the alphabet slow like
this genuine failure
of being here
together is enough

that's Monday

then on Friday what's been
done are abecedarian booms
your line moves into
all the excavations
ending in terror

types of terror:
comment, no comment
earth not ground
root not seed
fall, spring

the interdisciplinary species
chain reaction
chases distraction

Blind concourse

Spiritual seduction   place of execution
deduced by the hour   off tune ditty off duty
'curiosities with their traduced obligations'
concave vexations approaching meaning
spare circles, usurp spoken syllables
present in the hand's open contracts
A broken alphabet heals itself
through touch, wind through trees
expresses desire, pollen
clouds torn open

Abstracted by August's nervous heat
and foreign notions of aperture
entered into without rancor
Proceeds, whiter and greener, local
tongue's slippery inclines cede
interest to verticals or blind concourse
shuffled among tree-lined streets
from an ordinary imagination, less a place
than a tight grip on possibility, conditional
recognition in expressions of desire left
later taken as pollen
clouds tearing
open

Flickr

Origin. Beginning of days, initiate. Thought,
then word. Words charging after thought are
compulsive, mandatory. Expression is
obsessive. Ions fueled by kiss of sexy letters.
Is. Is. Listen to it hiss.

I take air with smoke how to hold that
cloud as it changes, is changing from
the animal it was / I was to become.

Long sky reaches its limit that's breath,
I can hold it closer than any thing

she writes inferring a body is home,
rest between phrases while torn bits
phase from breath, pixilate divisions,
separate to dimly visible flares.

That's science.

I don't care what you call it.

That's opinion.

If reticulation is continuous
there's nothing angry in this
red magnitude instead
its power merely whelms.

Problem of an undermind undermines
unusual determinations become core but
the atmosphere into which they disappear
less renaissance than meteorologic.
Problem of a moment
disclosing holes and

words conducting their own
conversation sign out to me
as I walk: "Try my beer in frozen glass."
Corona, high-energy light, magnetic
interactions between particles and
nights inhaling cocktails at Land's End
before a fire. Thanks
for the memories.
Then blink.

Midnight drains to zeros,
its digital construction.
Two sets of nothing
ratified by a colon.

In ornate defiance of the ordinary

The it key makes a click
on summer-warm pavement. Falls
as if fallen. The it key makes a
pavement sound and summer shines on it.
Pallid gestures trail behind. What's left
in leaving them? What's left is in
leaving them. Gone.

Six storeys over crushed plastic cups I blanched out a handful of dialog. After the initial
doing, what was difficult had grown to metronomic idiocisms and all my life from that
height was a dizzying joke I could no longer laugh through. I walked the Gran Via and I
shone like a traffic light. I talked into my dead cellphone blasting abstract plumes of
wet breath into cold dead air. My ears were dead. My nose was dead and a car tried to warn
me of its approach but I wasn't here. It wasn't the first time. I looked at the Christmas
lights and smiled. One pure moment.
Total presence.
But I was an idiot, and everything I did or didn't do was proof of how far a person will
go. Okay, climb out of that squash sump. There's a language I can almost tolerate.
There's me in a bar laughing. It's the second night of the new year so maybe there's
time.

Brick.
I don't know what poetry is anymore. An inadequate sequence of words cling desperately
to something central to generate other possibilities. As for the fictions, those slept
around the blocks. Before I boarded the plane, or felt my time up. Why not be kind,
useful? Why not neutralize complications in hard work, mopping, and buckets? Even
thinking the dull, except to judge confusing a twixt that doesn't mix an exercise in
boredom. So stutter in annoyance. Hard to get past the double consonant,
easier to fly to another continent.

Building nestled against a hill, scene pastoral and economic, estrogenic. The building makes me cry and causes severe cramping, slight spotting. I know it's not my home.

I walk into a small corner of the day's arabesque
an orientalism heavily patterned, detail and address
reflected back in ornate defiance of the ordinary,
sun angled across the sum of a room, transparent.

Priorities, like a large intake of breath.
Oh why not just be satisfied with breathing then.
With following along in the scheme of living moments
when what joins together joins. The actual
mostly unsaid and commentary reduced
to weather, sun or not, health, and ideas of liberty.

A limping dog wastes its efforts on this street
of businesses closed for the afternoon.

I walk into a small corner of the day
where the losses are less apparent

the dress rehearsal of former selves
not the wine-drunk one behind a tree
but the same scenario of a text supported
in stages by a motor that turns.

One moment the living room, the next,
the screened-in porch. My mother in pearls
and a sleeveless cream blouse with turquoise trim
the day my sister turned sweet sixteen and it's
late August 1965, a Hawaiian luau. My job is
to set the scene. To answer the door and
dance to the music in my first bikini
shake my so-far nonexistent hips.
The party's girls dressed up wearing makeup,
hair hardened with spray. Pastel silk shoes
kicked off and laughter, a "riot." But the joke
doesn't sustain, as the poem past can't either.

Even perfect people have problems

The day's corner is just a triangular relief
from all those other hours. The corner
an irritation, a place where illusions dissolve,
where the bikini's elastic legholes leave ugly marks,
pineapple punch burns the tongue.

The corner is where what's never said
        piles up, well-tended conical hills atop tables
                passed daily in the spice markets of
                        later's Mexico or Morocco, before.
                                Turmeric yellow and saffrony orange
                                dioramas.

Someone's deep purple remembered, another
copper value unwound. Yields.

          I go to the other planet which is world
outside the books, where there's
no imprint, where there are no
girls in broad headbands eating
institutional potatoes, or phones
ringing, rinky-dink tones announcing
messages received. Where every thing
twists apart from its english. Which is quieter
and more itself than any other place.

          Priorities like a large intake of breath
          Oh why not just be satisfied with breathing then.

I go to the Place of Water
an actual street on an actual map
where water once ran to the river Darro.
The kerbs are river stones
worn smooth by constant crossage.

          My blue escape flames. To love
          the glittering fixed forms
          and transport.

          Difficult to write about water.

Green foamy ocean brew below fog-heavy air on the coast and wind, yeah some.
Two figures backlit by blazing sun through clouds on water is glare,
an apostrophe'd hour between vowels.

Fire intoxicates proving the vigor of phantom light. Salt. Burning the outlines.

How to live without everything
I'm used to. Without a book
I'm nothing I once thought
laughing. Is this the same
as severing the intimacies of exaction?

I go far away. Past the laughter
past the noise past the funk.

My blue escape flames.
The figures tower in the distance.
Distance is doubt, hesitation,
a large intake of breath and firing on despite –

All my life I wanted
phrased inhesitantly
because.
I'm in the other

ether

okay, world

not stranded
but no standards
dictating
yet cognates not
the only falsehoods

some united states of me
shattered
open

where I feel the divine as mine
       mined the trajectories
              pasts and paths through
                     or behind
                          round yellow ands and
                              forgotten blue ofs

Of late nights and girls talking, a smoke, glasses of wine.
       Talk about the indispensable becomes *imprescindible* and
       what's to understand without the consonants?
       This other continent. This southern location exactly
       stretched open in its lingering enunciation. *To' pa' na'*.
       All for nothing.
       Dentro de nada.
       Inside of nothing.
       Vacío. Empty.

I go to this other country which is world
I go to this other world without my books
I go to this other world slung between
running dialog, bilingual, in my head
& each thought stands for two or more
the twixt ungenerous at first
with everyone
harder to get over
to the other
and with time
abstracted, abstract.

      The great poles of this beyond
      less vertical
      Concentric

      The coda
      repeats

      Cold air seeps
      closer.

      I go inside the world
      which is words

I've been here before
I sit

The poem's lies
crook and spit

I dream the holes
through
to a detail
held with heart

art gave me
permission
to generate.
Away from
the questions
and answers
into a space
that's open
uncompromised.

It's what I wanted
not to blame

Noh

the objects aren't objects
I object to the objects
little stupid pail
dusty black cigarette butts
why not draw them but
then she said "remember
your buddhism"
so I took some breath
and gave it back slowly
you could see it
smile the opening neck
unclenched but I object
to the picture the picture
has no object
and what did she mean
anyway?

Fast forward

Beethoven glows in the dark. Time embraces itself, arms unevenly akimbo trace slow circles in doo wop while refrigerator hums. I create new memories. Sun projects jagged shapes onto purple wall. Cat's eyes blaze red. A flying orange mouse with part of its tail missing sends her airborne right behind. It's dead. She's in heaven. Scant few hours to go 'til sun yells orange. Then it floats. Sizzles.

Duration as much illusion as anything else. So let's take a slow boat to China. All the time I felt no content cont(in)ent was passing. Peel me an orange. Peel me a grape. Window unfills an entire south wall, afternoon catches fire. Another false alarm.

I listen to a quartet in complete alignment with the horns, piano's hesitation. They kick me out. I roll forward in domino. Now's the part with triplets. She says she's an actress, her sister a poet, their other sister throws dice in a casino. Standing at the bar all bets on.
Water in tall blue bottles wiggles.

Serendipity. Kismet. It's the mind that swings. Not that hard to find. But you have to creep around or it parts like Budapest. TV screen flicker diffuses over stairwell opposite window. Kiss my lips. Grind my hips. Neighbors clawing themselves out from some cave, the sound turned off. To posit a theory regarding distances covered, what yet remains, an other entity invokes the third person, writing: "It is treasured." Peculiar gravity dispenses with personal pronouns, as if surrendered from a god, nonetheless invites the reply: "to whom?"

Currents

The hand, something arthritic. Heart, a scar. Music strands us in the deep, in shingled planes of animal sleep, wishbone, nomenclatured claims. Applause stalks in footfalls, in rain, thousands of notes in their own ink. Repetition past the point of amnesia can make this new. A sequence scatters and breathes. Breeds. This too. A reason is a grain of rice, a hard beginning.

In the accordion hours that fill with air and demands, individual and distinct, whistling sounds quaver and pierce, or forget to pierce and simply shiver. Wheeze.

I am afflicted by my own misunderstandings, have no patience for explanations. The voice of reason broadcasts over this foreign radio. A moment of radical silence gaps the airwaves. We're all waiting for a sign. Thought empties delivery what remains in place of eloquence. Then an orchestra begins. We're all prisoners of the same dream, its yoking effect scored upon the muses of our integrity. Violins and value, sparkling jewels in the crystallizing void. And crystals, the diamonds of our ancestral vacuums. When it rains there is understanding. The air smells clean, is itself; transparent. Slight nod to French horns.

Brazilian melody syncopates, rain, and now sudden sun shines through fast-moving mammatus clouds. You get the drift as their anvils discharge obsequious packages.

The light is provocative, sexily clean this morning as it brushes the edges of stone buildings in perfectly graced kisses. Birds are exuberant and want to sing. They sing.

Hands, less arthritic, want to tap out the rhythms connecting in my brain. They type. Body, curved in composition or full repose, carves the space necessary to occupy this moment that crosses time with space. When I cross time with space I get no equations. I get a well-tempered music that hints of structure and sequence. There is no way to divide the whole. It resists permissions, its will will not do. All my compromises are evident when I lift myself from my seat and take a step. I walk slow but feel no hesitation, I feel air expand in currents, draw some of it in.

Chispa

hands on my hymn
to know the gracious
inside, out as other
unruly as coincidence,
this untamed marriage
of portraits like planets
I carefully copy the text of our paths
as if I could prevent their collision
while even from this distance
I smell sparks

Passing the dark during evening spaces

Impact of bar lighting on digital photo
Photo screened on his cellphone To the
phone he presses her numbers Her number
one reason is his number one desire Is that
desire? Or control? Control yourself she
thinks The sentence goes on as lines of ink
implicate other details What she thinks to
him it matters

A man in the act of love A man in the way
of presence that to be taken pleasured want,
fell into push of pure fall Wind-scattered
fragments free the occlusions Hands to
grab for leaves circling their trees in the
swirl Your mouth, she had her desire,
swallowing His hunger, tasting her touch
his broken fast, dominion

That roses bud wild in me

and I drunken
amnesia devoured
by the tiniest petal
silence searing open eyes
and vertigo where
I call you
my obliteration
my speech
woman of disappearances
to speak of mutual dedications
delicate, trespass of garden
evasion, night's heart
reciprocal
tenderness and
trembling
ignorant as speech
still
distilled

Auspice

Habitually long passages pocketing
black metal glass register unguents
of slow shard metabolized toward
habits of feeling Welcome change

Arms to explain or insinuate what's
not consequent, sequence / not just

Absence degrees black
that nothing drops into
well maybe some consonants
while on these streets anyone can see
how dawn's apiary defines a park
worn marble facades decree
less, morning blue
stretch not imagination

From any or every location
it's not possible to replicate
the feelings part of reason

Lorca's face painted large
on red tour bus sides idles past –
gitanas hawk rosemary plumes
to jostling pedestrians
threatening fortune

Coral planet

A thin track of downy light value
in the where that was in rust
with no language or currency
crossing Atlantic pressures
strange, then pleasures so
little in common   Mars,
thorny coral planet swims closer
dangerous, reaches deep,
blood-slower than a close dance
in a Spanish bar Not even a tourist
and too eager to catch less
than distinguish beyond afternoon
sight, a cliff, but would be safe –
masks fallen off to the sides
Sitting in chairs praying with breath
held through the back door Chance
to look again after diving, and so filled,
navigating thinnest divides of skin
Tangled vines blind trust values
and use situations complicate by currents,
forced air, wholly absent yet conscious

Double yellow lines

Parking lots live in the caves of the homeless. We know the dogs who
lard their underground void. Olive air deposits trenchant and personal.
You have to sing to this clan to make ethnicity work, hammer their
coppers to dazzle their domes. Mistrust equals less parley vu dowsing for
fossils. Some live by the gun. Others hurl Miocene pebbles at the double
yellow lines outside their imaginations. You can't unhinge each exile
from its vacuum. So what can you call it? Imagination and delusion?
Imagination Andalusian? Imagination and illusion? Careful. I lived there.

Defense being offense

Dictums shriek don't fuck
with me I've got 51
brothers and sisters.
Locality's something
one slides into despite
busted deflectors.
Between the 58th and 59th
mention of terror
rain slits neon green leaves
with tropical force though
this isn't the tropics, this rain
just rain. Wet threads stray from
none-the-worse broken news,
washed-up flotsam, a sheltered head
and someone's shoulders blunt the jolt
terror effects, make-believe fragments
raze elegance. O sentinel warrants
against this search for our interests!
This isn't the tropics and the rain is just.
Listen to the applauding leaves.

Shine

Unrelentless hunger clouds future targets so that later's rendezvous
appeal's so distant. Reek of tall grass reeks of wild onion
and so forth. You're in the hold upon the matted arnica.
Rice is six feet high and bountiful so tall you simply walk
the rows invisible to anyone shorter than 6 foot. To god
you are transparent no matter how high the fanning stalks.
Inside scattered huts women prepare rice and men
tower from small platforms in the fields. They shout,
hurl stones at birds mesmerized by rice, deadstill mid-flight.
But enough of these veils: here comes your target.
In the same breath my own nucleus fastens to these couplets
this niche proves timely. If its grace doesn't cut it
clamp your teeth around your tongue. Only a fraction of
our selves remains young. When you roll back the scene
it always seems to rain. This recharges the cycle.
The treasure's in the depth of the deposits,
how deep you fold the seeds. Down here where
no one bothers us
shine.

As seen from above

If philosophy isn't dry then a cock is hard, expectant. If a cock isn't hard then there's no baton. There's silence. Over there is that a. Nothing. Message caned by wind. Zen koan involving a hand. Single lip marinated by a tongue.

After the foxes leave fewer peanuts jut from anthill-shaped mounds inside a grid rent by twigs and crenels drawn in Dogon sand. As all things, they concoct a picture. Perhaps the crops will come late. What crops? Peanut crops. More peanuts foretelling more impossible futures. But wind too parts the sands and topples remaining shells and nuts spelling the recent arrival of visitors. White men or men in white cloth. Like Jesus, not like Jesus.

Sly is what sly does. Furtive. Artful. The portents of autonomy constructed by hands abetted by cunning. An equation that employs animal and instinct in the same sentence, wand. Human and bestial ornamentally joined whereas anthropologically, separated by a digit, a folded hand.

Digital hours pass minute by precise minute. A girl in a green dress passes minutes in strolling from location A to location B. Where is location B? If a first staircase answers necessity, a second's invented by wit. Going up or coming down embody different actions. Distinct intentions. The intention of narrative: to carry, which may be used with across, through, on, under, over, an aggregation of prepositions to suggest transport may follow though the staircase will be rendered too thick with traffic to bear such instructions if no single one is selected. Better to build another staircase. Or a temple, a Mayan temple, stairs would lead to the pinnacle of a pyramid, resemble a diamond as seen from above. In diamond-studded hours before sleep, during sleep. Inside the diamonds of sleep with the shit of the day washed away by something wet. Springful. Young. Green.

All that shines on it shines from it. All that mirrors that all. Globe. Roundness. Human. Apt.

2B

or not

was a probable question.

The construction of the known world is a constant debacle. An entropy guided by hope, fierce hallucination fielding power. An inquiry addresses how we come to intersect such places.

Place is. Being where one is. Where one puts oneself, asserts full articulation. Dissimilar from reiterate. Verbalized by wind. Beginning soft. Blue wheel sky and granulated earth ground to fine dust. When I say blue I think russian with a p. Slow light glazes the powdered treatment of crystals. Articulates gestures time's passing folds into, shivers.

Boxes

that the whole was
inner and they wept
singing golems for
war is not the realm
of how what responds
nor its cancer

shifty purse sieves
other perils behind
wrong idea plants
parting operations

maximum jolt failure
efforts the basketed
plunge and light the
long day down its
breath our lungs
expunging

wake to less primary
dilution grip cleating
resistible granules as
generosity exchanged
filters code of
incidentals

Plexus

Nearly half July. Knowable things
can be divided into the obvious
the slightly obscure and the very
obscure. Reasons pass like seasons.
In the same way the cosmos has nothing
to say to us. That's not its problem.
That's our problem.

Distances

You trust at the corners, the truth a viable joke, its tremolo a minor chord. Your gaze is correct, you have the funky rhythm. You circumnavigate the airwaves, wing on high, tone in shaft. You strike the position, your virtue towers along the cobblestone walkway while you talk a violet streak, disperse a multitude of vitamins.

The light grills you. You have only questions. Prestidigitation. Your blue presence fuses into afternoon above the mountains. The light is yours, the orange and delirium. False cognates speak their own kind of music tangled between understandings. The difference between live and leave is greater than a shortened vowel.

I admit to moments without applying their gentle distress. A fly's wing. A hammer.

Having decided several things this morning I scribe them here:
The operation: an excess
The Cat bifurcates. It's not much but it's something.
This cold is irrational.
It's an occupation that affords me no small measure of unenjoyment.
Hard to begin, harder to continue.
I continue.

Utopian pile of thought an end in itself. Endpoints of spontaneity and emptiness, happy for nothing.

Twelve visible squares of darkening blue contrast with the ambience of radiated heat, hot beverage and orange cushions this side of them.

Presence of light-bearing abundances be they rectangular articulations or squared is in any case suffice it to say self and other, that yellow piece of fuck.

The cold is foreign, unwelcome invader but illegally resident. *Soy extranjera. Vengo de extranja.* And the tolerable damage, so be it, however sustaining the truth of excess.

Separation grows in life, or growth lives in separations, duplicities accelerate (cell division), augment. What's meant by "Conferring denies nothing, nor an abrogation."?

Ignorance mistakes misplaced gestures or Ignorance. Mistakes. Misplaced. (Gesture).

One mimes, carriaged in enchantment. Why do these words forget the accents of a kiss? Contemplate you, your nerves, the endings. He or she, the same. Forget nothing. There I was.

I didn't forget to have or have not. I bluntly refused it she says over coffee. Truth was one could live, remain a confused uncertainty pulled at by hope, optical illusions, sedimentary arrangements at the bottom of a cup.

The feeling in exile beyond love is ecstatic. Speech the love of the insane. You dream it. A comfort event. It falls from being. Its fall a sort of failure.

For its part, beyond the fact-free, some three of facets. From their something to unconsidered attachments, appearances and disappearances, breathing a kiss in warm yellow engagement. This.

Exhaling its human scorch, that yellow piece of fuck.
Sometimes to reject speech is to love well words.
The operation: an excess.
The Cat bifurcates. It's not much but it's something.
This cold is irrational.

Resists evasions, constricted maps. Her treasured darkness shaken from his
lips. He wouldn't say a word that wouldn't write. I spoke. I will. I trajectorize
in circular formations, plow deeper in.

Night sitting in her quiet sentence among crushed blue icicles. She hummed
the rests. Inertia held them in temporary resist. Or they embraced pushing
all their weight towards its edge. I spoke to each other. I rolled with
the mistranslations what was dangerous.
Oscillated risks and yellow fleck of kiss.

It's hard enough to begin, that much harder to continue.
We continue.

I only unhinge her, there's no display. You're called phrase, body, and.
The cold is foreign, unwelcome invader, illegally resident.
We weave between lengthening distances,
appearing and disappearing.
Touch in all that rages. Threadbare trusts.

Café Lisboa

The projected universe begins at this awning
Fernando's Hideaway on the accordion.
Every day I go to heaven with enormous speed.
When you say the hits keep coming I think
radio or war? I drug myself in the usual way.
TV screen explodes a car from its wall.
Coppery scarf trusses birds in trees
tan young shoulders escaping sleeves.

Benediction

Letters flutter above a page in quiet meditation in Mediterranean drifts.
Upward or downward sweep of circling air rearranges the letters until they
form sounds. If words play with each [thought, if thought depends on breath]
breath. If I dream with random precision. If verbs recycle like thought, not
like thought, which, having no center, ebbs, drifts. If thought changes.
[Recycles as breath, exactly as breath]
Words swim. Liquid as thought, stropped. Dense.

Carve land. Carry water. Air surrounds. [If life is mythical fire soon appears
signaling that things are about to heat up. Okay, so] Later fire appears,
flames fed by air as words paint each breath. Watch the striations of color and
custom habit their tepid struggles warming to thought
blossoms.

Watch the temperature rise observe how it heats the flowering molecules.
Expansion exacts dispersals. Again, thought blossoms. Motion in all moments
extol the moment.
Observed pollen bursts. [Mind the heat]

There is no story that is not true. The world has no end, and what is good
among one people is an abomination with others. There are strangers
everywhere. Strangers who stray from their clan on their way to where things
are or aren't the same.

A full week of processions, horns, percussion – now a rag-tag orchestra –
[listen to the trombone's notes slide from its cavity] dominates a cobblestoned
domain lit by perseverance. The penitents follow. Mournful mouthful.
Narration as blessing.

Week of saints. If with the passing of days penitents and bystanders drink the streets swallow or not an extraordinary quantity of body and other fluids. Weak of saints, the distance from church pew to trough, street.

The penitents follow. Some wear cone-head masks above satin robes to hide their identity. Others, less shameful, merely drink to forget their identity. Optical illusions, guarded confessions. Remorse. Incognito.

Jesus sexy on his cross, legs spread, arms open, worldly embrace? Penitence follows penis envy in the dictionary.

God's rays project through the lowering cloud mass alighting on rooftops and allegories, parabólicas and cables, tops of newly flowering trees. Lines thusly joined refute penetration. A geometry of incognizant shapes rent, meridian points intersect.
What's human? The answer is the question.

As scraggly orchestra members limp off towards the edges of the city clouds part, seduced by temptation. Sun pricks through and men in lime-green plastic suits armed with enormous plastic bags, carrying big mops, scatter from the main avenues into all the sidestreets, alleyways, and plazas of Granada to begin their work. Messages code and uncode. Pass from one to an other. All we know just as we know it. Think we know it. Thought blossoms! Erase from these streets! Amen.

Stop. Continue.

"I concede. Life has no meaning." They laugh godlessly. Pause. Wince. It's an old show. Circle in a square and seats all around. Spectacle. Lights, and surround silence that returns the suiteness.

Broken by ease, broken by oh let's not start with the brokenness please too many generations of uselessness and invention that dis-invite curiosity. The moments pass then something at the heart of no heart gives pause. Enzymes. Estrogen. Man o man.

Candles that don't illuminate so much as approximate the area, the darkness around this thing aglow. Big, yellow, and covered with paint. A man's face suffuses in soft strokes that radiate from the top of his head generating consonants. Another version, his animal twin, teeth bared, grins back at him.

The painter writes
at the end there is a happy end
I paint a king on a throne
laughing and laughing, big,
cause I think we all have
inside that gold and that is
reason we still are
living do you know?

I write back, *"sigues!"*
no longer paused at
cease and desist!

The master recycler puts her shoulder to the wheel

There is no time. It is stooped and frail.
However, am glad to be alive. The apparitional
single phrase: echo she is the knowledge he was
after, wasted, not what he was expecting, it could be
to torment your graces, expressed, is
to value them; do them no harm no harm
to anything, constantly, dispassionately, inevitably
free to be nothing or nothing in particular,
consider the griefs in trying to be special.

Acoustics

When I get to eternity let me
slip into something comfortable
and if there are snake charmers
I won't be a snake, no, I'll
be the same ragged princess
as always, up late archiving
the astroturf fielding gods.
A name's collective shelters
zones of prohibition so liberate
the 15,000 visions, uteral & fallopian
animal commerce in skin. Touch
skirts reason, vets the mantic
psychology of objects,
emboldened by their
shapely level.

A poet and artist, Laurie Price has been writing and making visual work for a few decades. She was awarded a Gerbode Foundation Poetry grant and subsequently began her life as a citizen of the world at large. She is the author of one full-length poetry collection, *Except for Memory* (Pantograph Press, Berkeley, CA) and four chapbooks, *Going On Like This* (Northern Lights Int'l Poetry / Brooklyn Series, Brooklyn, NY), *Under the Sign of the House* (Detour Press, Brooklyn, NY / e-book, readme), *The Assets* (Situations Press, NY) and *Minim* (e-book, Faux Press, MA / Tokyo). Her on-going visual work / photos are posted here: graciouseconomiesandcorrugatedshadows.blogspot.com and her collages / assemblages have been exhibited in SF, CA, Mexico and Spain.